ISLINGTON

Homes

Nicola Baxter

W
FRANKLIN WATTS
LONDON • SYDNEY

Some people live in the countryside.
Their nearest neighbours or shops
might be a long way away.

3

Some people live in a town or city.
There are many homes and shops
and places where people work nearby.

What kind of place do you live in?

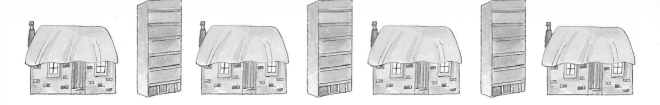

There might be just one home
in a house or bungalow.
Inside a block of flats or a skyscraper,
lots of people live in separate homes.

Try this later
With your friends, paint lots of boxes
and pile them up to make a very tall building.

Some homes can move from place to place!

When it is cold, your home can keep you warm.
When it is wet, your home can keep you dry.

11

Inside a home there is somewhere to get food ready.

What are these things used for in a kitchen?

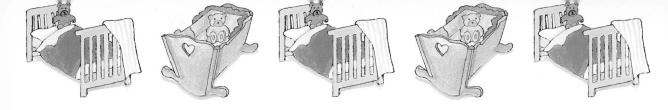

A home has places for everyone to sleep and somewhere to keep yourself clean. What other kinds of rooms do homes sometimes have?

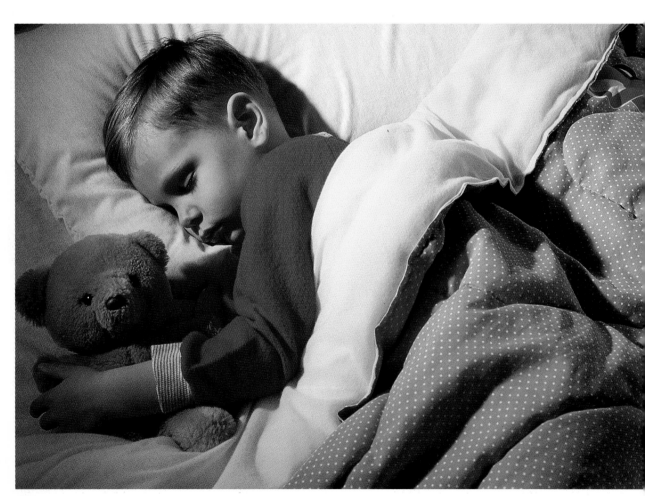

There are shelves and cupboards and
drawers where all sorts of things
can be kept.

17

If someone moves house, they often need a huge truck to carry all their things to their new home.

Home is a good place to relax with your friends and family.

Who do you spend time with in your home?

Wherever you live, home is...

where you come home to!

Index

This edition 2003
Franklin Watts
96 Leonard Street
London EC2A 4XD

Franklin Watts Australia
45-51 Huntley Street
Alexandria NSW 2015

Copyright © Franklin Watts 1996
Editor: Sarah Ridley
Designer: Nina Kingsbury
Illustrator: Michael Evans

ISBN: 0 7496 5222 5

A CIP catalogue record for this
book is available from the British
Library.

Dewey Decimal Classification
Number: 728

Acknowledgements:
The publishers would like to
thank Carol Olivier and Stephen
Mabalot of Kenmont Primary
School for their help with the
cover of this book.

Photographs: Collections 20;
James Davies Travel Photography
5, 6, 11; Eye Ubiquitous 8;
Robert Harding Picture Library 3;
Images 12; Peter Millard cover;
ZEFA 9, 14.

Printed in Malaysia